THE SPECTACULAR SCIENCE of
ART

written by Rob Colson

illustrated by Moreno Chiacchiera

KINGFISHER
LONDON & NEW YORK

KINGFISHER
LONDON & NEW YORK

First published 2024 in the United States
by Kingfisher
120 Broadway, New York, NY 10271
Kingfisher is an imprint of
Macmillan Children's Books, London

ISBN 978-0-7534-7915-5

Distributed in the U.S. and Canada by Macmillan,
120 Broadway, New York, NY 10271

Library of Congress Cataloging-in-Publication
data has been applied for.

Author: Rob Colson
Illustrator: Moreno Chiacchiera
Consultant: Susie Hodge
Designed and edited by Tall Tree Ltd

Kingfisher Books are available for special
promotions and premiums.
For details contact:
Special Markets Department, Macmillan
120 Broadway, New York, NY 10271.

For more information please visit:
www.kingfisherbooks.com

Printed in China
2 4 6 8 9 7 5 3 1
1TR/1223/WKT/RV/128MA

EU representative:
1st Floor, The Liffey Trust Centre
117-126 Sheriff Street Upper,
Dublin 1 D01 YC43

MIX
Paper | Supporting
responsible forestry
FSC
www.fsc.org
FSC® C116313

CONTENTS

WHAT IS ART?

For thousands of years, people have created images of the world around them. Making art isn't just a matter of copying what we see. It is also a way to imagine how the world could be different. Art can help us to understand ourselves or just make us feel good.

CAN SCIENCE HELP ARTISTS?

Artists and scientists both try to make sense of the world around them. This means that science and art often work well together. A scientific understanding of how our minds work can help artists to create dazzling effects. Meanwhile, scientists use their imagination and creativity to come up with new ideas.

UNLOCKING THE UNCONSCIOUS

In the first half of the twentieth century, a group of artists called the Surrealists were inspired by ideas from the science of psychoanalysis. To explore their unconscious minds, the Surrealists invented a technique called automatism, combining images in unexpected ways in paintings and collages.

Working independently from the Surrealists, Mexican artist Frida Kahlo (1907–1954) also painted images from her imagination.

COLLECTIVE MEMORY

Artists often tell stories with their artworks. Indigenous people of Australia pass on stories from their past using an artform called Dreamtime. Dreamtime paintings are often highly stylized, using symbols to represent objects and events. "U" shapes represent people. Circles represent campsites or water holes, while straight lines may represent journeys undertaken by their ancestors.

YOUR BRAIN ON ART

When artists create artworks, their brains create new connections. Their stress levels fall and they find it easier to focus. Looking at artworks can also help our brains. By giving us new ways to see the world, looking at art makes us think in different ways. Today, art therapy is widely used to help patients to recover from strokes and other brain conditions.

Trained art therapists help people to express their inner thoughts and feelings through art.

CAVE ART

Some of the earliest artworks were made in caves. Working by firelight, artists used mineral pigments to create images ranging from simple handprints to spectacular hunting scenes.

LASCAUX CAVE

The Lascaux Cave in France was discovered by accident in 1940 by a teenage boy out walking his dog. The cave walls are covered in more than 2,000 paintings, including images of animals such as horses, mammoths, bears, and wolves. The paintings were created about 17,000 years ago.

The cave was closed to the public in 1963 to prevent damage to the paintings caused by the large number of visitors. Exact replicas of the artworks have been made, including The Hall of Bulls, a section of wall depicting a series of huge animals, such as a larger-than-life 17-foot-long bull.

Ancient artwork

The oldest known figurative artwork is a life-size painting of a wild pig found in Maros-Pangkep in Indonesia. Scientists have dated the artwork by examining a mineral deposit that formed over part of the painting. They discovered that the deposit is 45,500 years old, which means that the painting is at least this age, but may be much older.

Auroch (wild cattle)

Horse

CAVE OF HANDS

The Cueva de los Manos (Cave of Hands) is a cave complex in Argentina with artworks dating back 9,000 years. The paintings in the caves include a spectacular collage of more than 800 handprints. Most of the prints are stencils. Paint was sprayed around a hand using a bone pipe. About 95 per cent of the prints are left hands, suggesting that their creators used their dominant right hands to hold the pipe.

17-foot-long
bull auroch.

Deer

SCULPTURE IN THE ANCIENT WORLD

Many large sculptures made from stone or metal survive from the ancient world. These works were often made for religious purposes as decoration for temples.

BRONZE SCULPTURES

The metal bronze was first made around 5,000 years ago. Bronze is an alloy (mixture) made mainly of copper, mixed with smaller quantities of tin and other substances. Bronze is harder than copper, and it allowed artists to make large and detailed sculptures from metal for the first time.

Indian bronzes

Many of the oldest bronze sculptures in the world are found in India. Some of them date back more than 4,000 years. These intricate sculptures often depict Hindu gods.

Greek realism

The ancient Greeks created realistic, larger-than-life sculptures out of bronze. The sculptures were made using a technique called lost-wax. First, a non-bronze core was made that was almost the size of the finished work. This was covered in a layer of wax, which was covered in clay. The wax was melted out and molten bronze was poured into the space between the core and the clay. Once the metal had set, the clay was removed.

This bronze sculpture depicts the Hindu god Ganesha. He has four arms and the head of an elephant. Images of Ganesha are seen throughout India as he is believed to be a bringer of good luck.

This sculpture of the Greek goddess Artemis was made in the 4th century BCE.

EGYPTIAN MONUMENTS

Sandstone cliff

Four seated figures
of Ramesses II

Some of the most spectacular artworks that have survived from the ancient world are found in Egypt. The Egyptians carved huge stone statues as monuments to their pharaohs. The twin temples of Abu Simbel were carved into the mountainside in the 13th century BCE as monuments to Pharaoh Ramesses II and his wife Queen Nefertiti. Four 65-foot-high images of the pharaoh Ramesses II flank the entrance to the main temple.

Cranes lifted the
statues piece by piece.

RELOCATION

The temples at Abu Simbel were taken apart and relocated in 1964. This huge operation took four years to complete. Shortly afterward, the area was flooded by Lake Nasser, an artificial lake that had been created behind the Aswan Dam on the River Nile.

LINEAR PERSPECTIVE

Linear perspective uses math to give paintings a three-dimensional look.

ONE-POINT PERSPECTIVE

The simplest form of linear perspective is one-point perspective. Dutch artist Vincent van Gogh's painting *Bedroom in Arles* (1889) uses one-point perspective to create a sense of depth in his room.

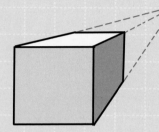

Vanishing point
Using linear perspective, parallel lines within a painting are shown to meet at a point in the distance known as the vanishing point, which lies on a horizontal horizon line.

Horizon line

Vanishing point

Parallel lines

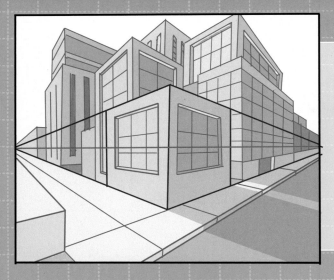

TWO-POINT PERSPECTIVE

Two-point perspective uses two vanishing points. For instance, in a scene looking at the corner of a building, each wall has its own vanishing point.

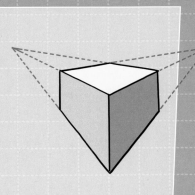

THREE-POINT PERSPECTIVE

Three-point perspective uses three vanishing points that form a triangle with the viewing point in the center. It is used when looking up or down at a scene.

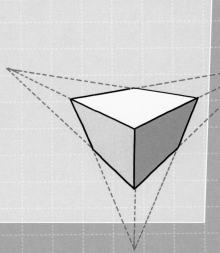

Filippo Brunelleschi

Italian architect and sculptor Filippo Brunelleschi (1377–1446) was the first person to work out an exact system of linear perspective. Brunelleschi studied the way that objects appeared to change size and shape when seen from different distances and angles. To demonstrate his ideas, he drew a scene using a grid to copy exactly what he saw square by square but in mirror image. He then invited people to compare the painting with the real scene behind it using a mirror, showing them how similar they were.

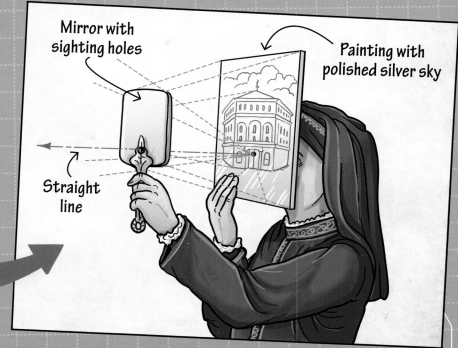

Mirror with sighting holes

Painting with polished silver sky

Straight line

THE ARTIST'S STUDIO

In fifteenth-century Europe, a period of artistic achievement known as the Renaissance began in Italy. Many Renaissance artists ran large studios, paid for by wealthy patrons. Aspiring artists started out as apprentices, called *garzoni*, learning every aspect of the artistic process from their masters over the course of several years. The apprentices would live with their masters at the studio and were expected to work long hours.

The master at work

PREPARING MATERIALS

Apprentices began training at about age 13, doing basic tasks such as grinding pigments. Artists used a variety of minerals and plants as pigments. Some colors were very expensive to make. For example, a deep blue color was made by grinding the gemstone lapis lazuli into a fine powder. For this reason, blue was reserved for the clothing of important figures such as the biblical Mary.

Drawing a statuette

LEARNING TO DRAW

The apprentices learned to draw by copying works by their masters and other renowned artists. They then moved on to drawing from statuettes. Finally, they were allowed to draw live models, often one of their fellow *garzoni*.

Background painter

PAINTING BACKGROUNDS

Large paintings were a group effort. More advanced students painted the less important parts of a painting, such as the landscape background, while the master painted the central figures. The students were trained to paint in their master's style, and sometimes whole paintings would be completed by the most talented pupils. Regardless of who painted the work, it would be signed only by the master.

MOVING OUT

Once he had proved himself with an original artwork that demonstrated his skill, an artist could move out of the studio and take on his own students.

Life drawing

ART AND ANATOMY

During the Renaissance, some artists studied human anatomy by dissecting dead bodies. The artists wanted to know how bodies worked under the skin in order to make more lifelike paintings and sculptures.

DETAILED STUDIES

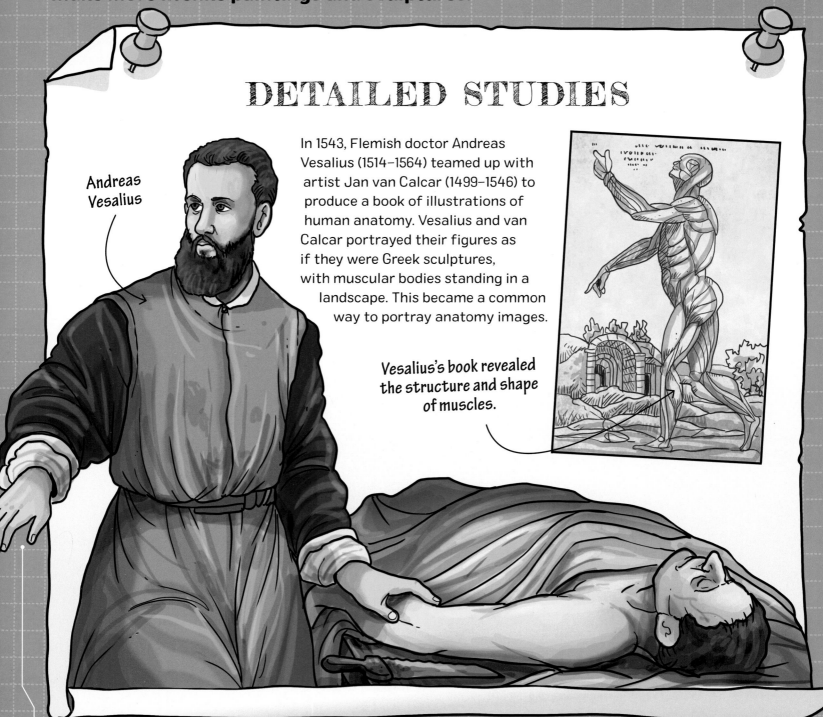

In 1543, Flemish doctor Andreas Vesalius (1514–1564) teamed up with artist Jan van Calcar (1499–1546) to produce a book of illustrations of human anatomy. Vesalius and van Calcar portrayed their figures as if they were Greek sculptures, with muscular bodies standing in a landscape. This became a common way to portray anatomy images.

Andreas Vesalius

Vesalius's book revealed the structure and shape of muscles.

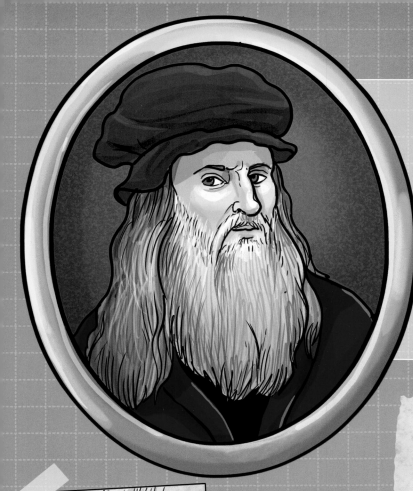

LEONARDO DA VINCI

Italian artist Leonardo da Vinci (1452–1519) produced hundreds of drawings of human anatomy. Like Vesalius, Leonardo depicted muscular bodies. He was fascinated by the way the skeleton is moved by the muscles attached to it. Also an accomplished engineer, Leonardo studied how forces acted on the bones. He also built models of organs to study how they worked.

Inner connections

Leonardo studied every bone and muscle group in the human body. This drawing reveals the inner workings of the human hand, showing how tendons connect the finger bones to the muscles in the arm that control them.

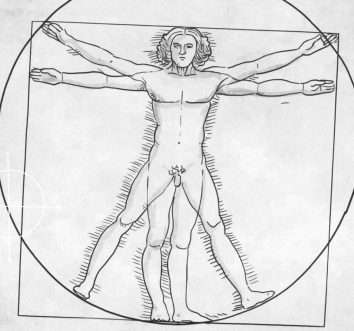

VITRUVIAN MAN

Bringing together art, science, and mathematics, Leonardo's drawing *Vitruvian Man* shows the proportions of a human body. The drawing has been copied by many artists.

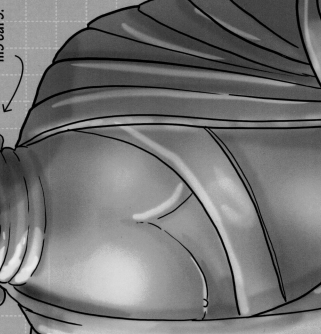
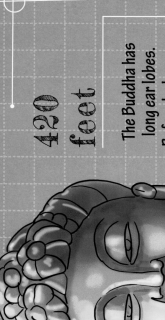

MONUMENTAL ART

420 feet

The Buddha has long ear lobes. *Before he became a teacher, he was a prince and wore heavy jewelry in his ears.*

Monumental art is made to impress. Giant statues are often placed in prominent places so that they can be seen from great distances. Made from bronze, steel, and gold, the huge **Spring Temple Buddha** in Henan, China, dominates the landscape around it.

This hand gesture is called the *karana mudra*. It is used by Buddhists during meditation.

WHO WAS THE BUDDHA?

Siddhartha Gautama, commonly known as the Buddha, was a religious teacher who lived in South Asia around 500 BCE. As the Buddhist religion spread across Asia, ornate statues celebrating the Buddha's life started to appear. Buddhists believe that time spent in front of a statue of the Buddha helps to create a calm mind.

In his left hand, the Buddha holds a lotus flower, which is a symbol of purity.

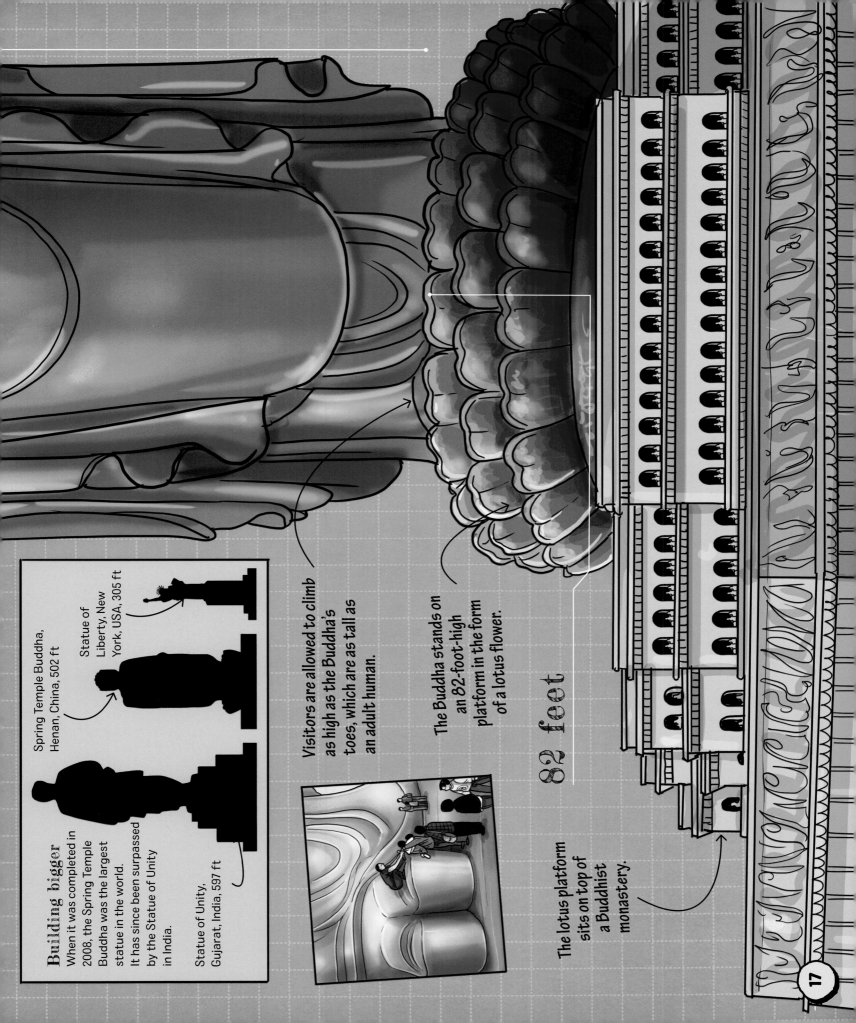

Building bigger
When it was completed in 2008, the Spring Temple Buddha was the largest statue in the world.
It has since been surpassed by the Statue of Unity in India.

Spring Temple Buddha, Henan, China, 502 ft

Statue of Liberty, New York, USA, 305 ft

Statue of Unity, Gujarat, India, 597 ft

Visitors are allowed to climb as high as the Buddha's toes, which are as tall as an adult human.

The Buddha stands on an 82-foot-high platform in the form of a lotus flower.

82 feet

The lotus platform sits on top of a Buddhist monastery.

COLOR THEORY

Artists study color theory to understand how color affects their work. The careful selection of colors from different parts of the visible spectrum can create stunning effects.

THE COLOR WHEEL

English scientist Isaac Newton (1643–1727) invented a color wheel on which all the colors of the rainbow are laid out in a circle. Newton thought that the rainbow contained seven colors: red, orange, yellow, green, blue, indigo, and violet.

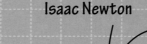
Isaac Newton

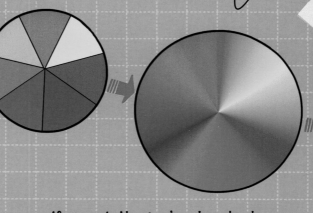

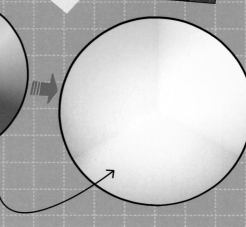

If you spin Newton's color wheel, you see the color white.

BUILDING A COLOR WHEEL

There are many different ways to make a color wheel. One way is to start with primary colors and build up from there.

Primary colors
Primary colors are three colors from which all other colors can be made by mixing them together. When artists mix paints, they start with red, yellow, and blue as their primary colors.

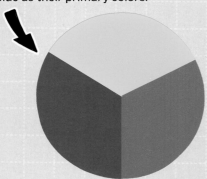

Secondary colors
Secondary colors are made by mixing equal amounts of two primary colors together. Red plus yellow makes orange, blue plus yellow makes green, and red plus blue makes purple.

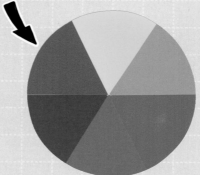

Tertiary colors
Tertiary colors are made by combining equal parts of primary and secondary colors. This makes 12 colors in total:
1 yellow, 2 amber, 3 orange, 4 vermillion, 5 red, 6 magenta, 7 violet, 8 purple, 9 blue, 10 teal, 11 green, 12 chartreuse

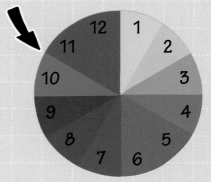

COMPLEMENTARY COLORS

Complementary colors are colors that sit on opposite sides of the color wheel. When placed next to one another, complementary colors enhance each other's intensity, creating bold, high-contrast images.

These red roses stand out against the complementary color green around them.

COLOR PHOTOGRAPHY

In 1903, the French Lumière brothers invented the first color photography, which they called Autochrome Lumière. The brothers passed light through filters made of colored starch grains to produce an image on a glass plate. They used vermillion, green, and violet as their primary colors. The plates were viewed by shining a light through them.

This Autochrome Lumière photograph was taken in Kyoto, Japan, in 1912.

ANALOGOUS COLORS

Analogous colors are colors that sit next to each other on the color wheel. When used together, they create a calming effect.

Van Gogh's painting of sunflowers combines the analogous colors yellow, orange, and green.

RGB or CMYK

Light-producing devices such as TV screens use red, green, and blue (RGB) as their primary colors. Printers use cyan, magenta, and yellow with the addition of black. This is known as CMYK (K stands for blacK). While a screen builds up color from a dark background, a printer subtracts color from a white background. Using RGB for printing would result in very dark images. Using the lighter CMY makes brighter images. Black ink is added to make dark colors, which are hard to make with CMY alone.

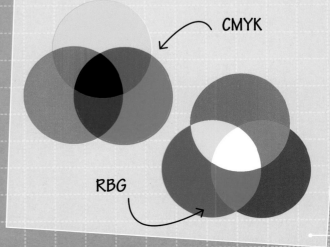

CMYK

RBG

LIGHT AND SHADE

Chiaroscuro, an Italian word meaning "light-dark," is a painting technique that uses strong contrasts between light and shade. This adds a sense of depth to paintings. It can also produce dramatic scenes that grab the viewer's attention.

ADDING DEPTH

The ancient Greek painter Apollodorus invented a technique called skiagraphia to create shadows in drawings using cross-hatched shading. The shadows give images an extra sense of depth.

EL GRECO

Greek-Spanish painter El Greco (1541–1614) used chiaroscuro to create shimmering shades in the folds of clothing. He made the effect even more dramatic by giving his figures exaggerated features such as elongated bodies and fingers. El Greco's dramatic style influenced 20th-century artists such as the Cubists (see page 37).

Oil paints

Renaissance artists developed chiaroscuro with the aid of new paints. Previously, painters had used paints such as egg-based tempera. These paints were fast-drying and difficult to blend. New oil-based paints were developed in the fifteenth century by mixing pigments with linseed oil. The oil paints dried much more slowly, allowing painters to build up their paintings with thin layers of paint. Artists could now blend gradual color tones and paint realistic chiaroscuro scenes.

ADDING DRAMA

Italian painter Caravaggio (1571–1610) developed an extreme version of the chiaroscuro technique called tenebrism. The subjects of Caravaggio's paintings are brightly lit by a single light source and their faces appear to glow against the black background.

In Caravaggio's *The Calling of Saint Matthew*, the figures are lit from a single light source to the right. The lighting focuses attention on the seated figures.

PORTRAITS

Portrait artists create recognizable paintings of individual people. Before the invention of photography, a portrait was the only way to record a person's appearance. Today, portraits remain a popular art form as it is a great way to capture a person's personality.

RECOGNIZING FACES

Faces can change a great deal over a person's lifetime, yet we can still instantly recognize someone we have not seen in many years. Our hair may change color, our skin may become wrinkly and we may put on weight, but we remain recognizably "us." A person's likeness depends on the spatial relationships between different features more than their shape or color. For example, the location of the eyes is more important than their color. Another aspect of faces that doesn't change over time is the shape of the skull.

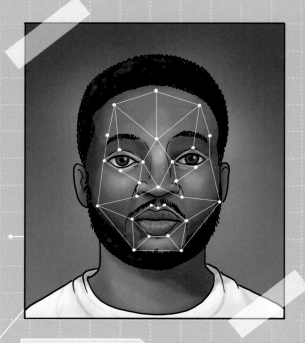

Making a faceprint
A computer recognizes faces by measuring features such as the distance between the eyes and the shape of the cheekbones. The computer turns these measurements into a set of points called a faceprint. Like our fingerprints, each of us has a unique faceprint. Many artists make similar measurements before they begin a portrait.

MONA LISA

Leonardo da Vinci's 1503 portrait the *Mona Lisa* captures his subject in a natural pose, as if she has just turned her head towards the viewer. Leonardo used a technique called sfumato to create a smoky effect in which the colors gradually shade into one another.

The figure sits in front of an imaginary landscape.

SELF-PORTRAITS

The Dutch artist Rembrandt van Rijn (1606–1669) painted self-portraits throughout his life. He painted himself while looking in the mirror so the paintings show a reverse image.

Rembrandt painted these self-portraits nearly 40 years apart. In the painting on the left, he is 24 years old, while he is 63 years old in the portrait on the right. He has changed from a young man to an old man, but the portraits are both recognizably him. The shapes of features such as the nose and the mouth remain distinctive.

Self-portrait from 1630

Self-portrait from 1669

RECORDING LIKENESSES

German artist Hans Holbein the Younger (1497–1543) painted this portrait of Christina of Denmark in 1538. He had been sent to Denmark by English King Henry VIII, who was looking for a new wife and wanted to know what Christina looked like. Although Henry liked the painting, the marriage did not go ahead.

Following the death of her first husband, Christina wears black mourning clothes.

GOING MOBILE

In the nineteenth century, a group of artists called the Impressionists created a new painting style by painting outside, known by the French term "en plein air." The artists captured the way that changing weather affected light and shadow across a landscape.

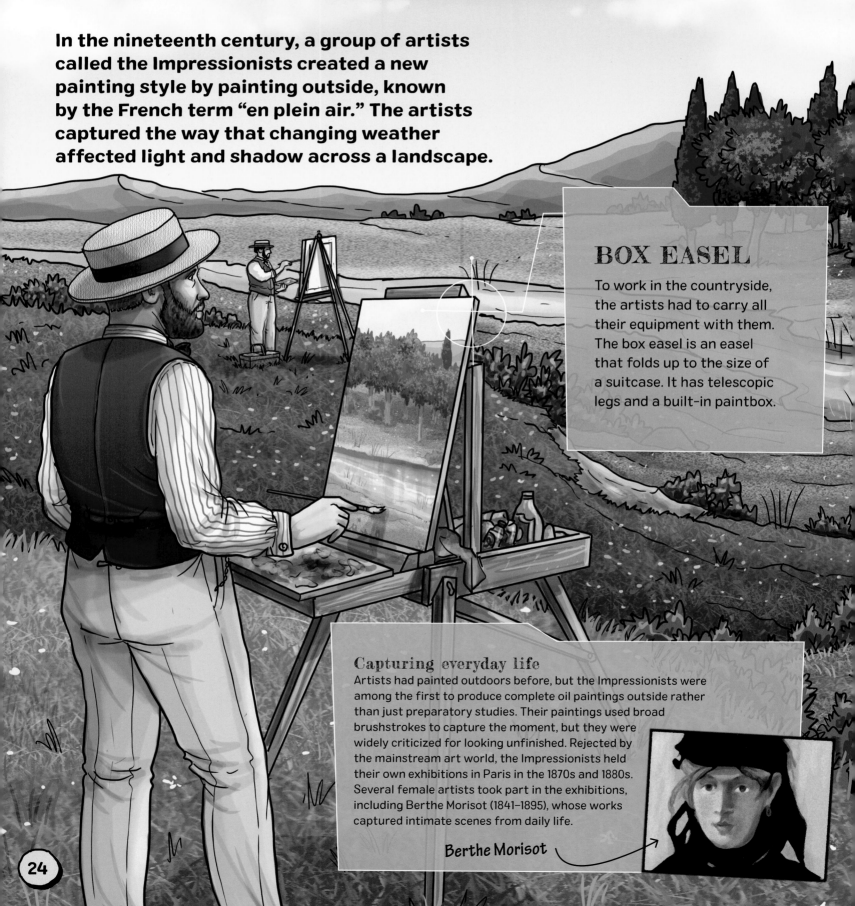

BOX EASEL

To work in the countryside, the artists had to carry all their equipment with them. The box easel is an easel that folds up to the size of a suitcase. It has telescopic legs and a built-in paintbox.

Capturing everyday life

Artists had painted outdoors before, but the Impressionists were among the first to produce complete oil paintings outside rather than just preparatory studies. Their paintings used broad brushstrokes to capture the moment, but they were widely criticized for looking unfinished. Rejected by the mainstream art world, the Impressionists held their own exhibitions in Paris in the 1870s and 1880s. Several female artists took part in the exhibitions, including Berthe Morisot (1841–1895), whose works captured intimate scenes from daily life.

Berthe Morisot

FLOATING ARTIST

French Impressionist Claude Monet (1840–1926) fitted out a boat as a floating studio so that he could paint from the river. Monet would often anchor the boat at one location to paint a scene, but sometimes he let it drift downstream to create a painting that included impressions of many different scenes.

A large umbrella protects against the sun and rain.

PAINT TUBES

The metal paint tube was invented in 1841 by American painter John Goffe Rand (1801–1873). The tin tubes prevented the oil paints from drying out, allowing painters to carry unused paint home with them. This made outdoor painting affordable for many more artists.

ARTIST COLONIES

Artist colonies emerged in many countries in the nineteenth century. Groups of artists would travel to a location together to paint scenes outdoors.

WOODBLOCK PRINTS

Between the seventeenth and nineteenth centuries, an artform called Ukiyo-e was developed in Japan. Colorful woodblock prints depicted scenes from everyday life, landscapes, and mythical creatures. Ukiyo-e's bold images inspired many artists around the world.

MAKING A PRINT

Woodblock print making involved a series of stages, each carried out by a highly skilled artisan.

FLOATING WORLD

Ukiyo-e means "pictures of the floating world" in Japanese. The "floating world" was the world of the theater districts in Japan's major cities. The flamboyant style of the actors and artists that lived in those areas made them style icons of their day.

1 Carving the image
To make a woodblock print, the artist first draws an image on paper. The paper is glued over a piece of wood and the artist carves the image into the surface of the wood to create a raised image called a relief.

ART FOR EVERYONE

While paintings were very expensive and could only be bought by a rich elite, woodblock prints were relatively cheap, and they became popular throughout Japan. The more colors were used, the more expensive the print. Landscape scenes were particularly popular as decoration for people's homes.

A view of Mount Fuji by Hokusai

2 Applying the ink
Ink is applied to the wood and paper is placed on top of it. A flat tool called a baren is rolled over the paper so that the ink is transferred from the wood block.

3 Adding colors
To make prints with many colors, the process is repeated using a series of woodblocks, each with just part of the whole scene on it.

RULES OF COMPOSITION

Composition refers to the arrangement of objects in an artwork, along with its lighting, shadows, and color combinations. Artists tell stories through their artworks. Knowledge of the rules of composition helps them to tell their stories as powerfully as possible.

In *The Scream*, by Norwegian artist Edvard Munch (1863–1944), the composition encourages the viewer to move their eye from the top left to rest on the focal point in the bottom right.

LEADING THE EYE

Leading the eye is a way of drawing the viewer's attention across an image from one place of interest to another. To create compositions that lead the eye, artists need to know how human perception works. We are attracted by areas with high contrast and hard edges, and we are drawn to look at irregular shapes. The eye can also be led through a painting by its linear perspective. When looking at a painting, we also need a place to rest our eyes at the end.

In this painting *Crashed Aeroplane*, by American artist John Singer Sargent (1856–1925), the two focal points are arranged according to the rule of thirds.

RULE OF THIRDS

The rule of thirds is a way of placing the most important parts of a painting at eye-catching places. The canvas is divided into nine equal parts by drawing two horizontal lines and two vertical lines. The focal points of the composition are placed around one of the four points where the lines intersect.

THE GOLDEN RATIO

In mathematics, the Golden Ratio is the ratio 1 : 1.618. It is produced by dividing a line in a particular way:

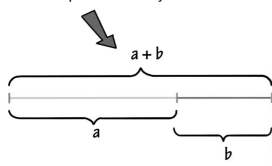

$a + b$

a

b

$$\frac{a}{b} = \frac{a+b}{a} = 1.618....$$

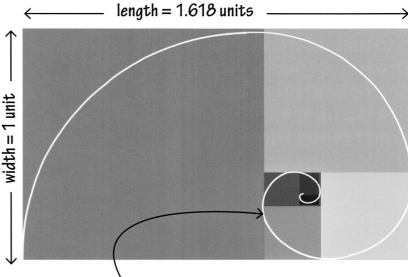

length = 1.618 units

width = 1 unit

Golden Spiral

In art, a rectangle with sides that are in the Golden Ratio is often thought to be pleasing to the eye. Divide the rectangle into smaller Golden Ratios and add a curving line to make a Golden Spiral.

GOLDEN SPIRAL IN ART

The Golden Spiral can be used to make a very effective composition. *The Great Wave* by Japanese artist Hokusai (1760–1849) is composed around a Golden Spiral.

The huge wave curves around a Golden Spiral.

OPTICAL ILLUSIONS

When we look at images, our brains perform a series of tricks to make sense of them. Artists can fool our brains by creating optical illusions, which make us see things that aren't really there.

HOLBEIN'S SKULL

Painted in 1533 by Hans Holbein the Younger, *The Ambassadors* portrays two wealthy men dressed in fine clothes. Across the bottom of the painting is a strange gray splash of paint. To make sense of the splash, the viewer needs to stand to the right of the painting, at which point it transforms into a human skull. Holbein achieved this effect using a technique called anamorphic perspective.

Ambiguous images

Artists often play with ambiguous images. These are images that we can see as one thing or another thing, but not as both at the same time. Is this a picture of a duck or a rabbit?

The skull looks like this when the painting is viewed from the right.

OP ART

Optical illusion art, or Op Art for short, is an artistic movement that started in the 20th century. Op artists play with their viewers' perceptions, making them believe that they are seeing more than is actually there. British artist Bridget Riley (born 1931) creates paintings of wavy lines and spirals that appear to move before your eyes.

Light or dark?

When we look at an image, we expect certain features to appear. For example, an object in the shade should be darker. Take a look at this image and compare the two squares marked **A** and **B**. Can you believe that they are exactly the same color? You probably need to cover the rest of the image to check.

When you look at this image from the corner of your eye, do the circles start to turn?

IMPOSSIBLE SHAPES

Dutch artist MC Escher (1898–1972) played with perspective to create scenes with impossible shapes, such as staircases that appear to go up forever.

DIGITAL ART

Digital art is art made using computers. The artworks may be created by drawing on a screen using a tablet or a mouse, or the computer may generate the art itself after being given a set of rules to work to.

COMPUTER-AIDED ARTISTS

Today, many artists work digitally using programs such as Photoshop. This allows artists to combine different media such as drawings and photographs and create new effects. The artists draw directly on the screen using a digital stylus.

ARTIST-AIDED COMPUTERS?

Between the 1970s and his death in 2016, British artist Harold Cohen (1928–2016) developed a series of computer art programs called AARON. The computer was linked to a robotic painting machine, which painted the images on the canvas. Cohen's goal was to make AARON draw the way Cohen drew. Over the years, it improved to the stage where it was able to paint realistic images of people.

PRIZE-WINNING COMPUTER

AI (Artificial Intelligence) involves computers that are able to learn. In 2022, the winner of the Digital Art prize at the Colorado State Fair was a painting of a sci-fi fantasy scene. It later emerged that game developer Jason Allen had made the image using AI program Midjourney. Allen uploaded a selection of images to the computer, which combined the images in a new way. Allen was allowed to keep the prize, but the award sparked a debate as to whether or not a computer can truly be creative.

FIRST PLACE

FINE ARTS

COLORADO STATE FAIR

PUEBLO, CO

AI art generators even allow you to make artworks on a smartphone.

MULTIMEDIA ART

Digital artworks often include the use of video. Modern art galleries today often feature video installations in which artists use huge screens to immerse the viewer in a new experience. These are known as multimedia artworks as they combine more than one kind of medium, such as images and sounds.

American artist Joan Jonas (born 1936) was a pioneer in multimedia art in the 1960s. Her works combine video, sounds, and drawings with live performance. She is also known for the playful use of mirrors in her art.

INSPIRED BY NATURE

Many artists have been inspired by the beauty of nature, none more so than Dutch artist Vincent van Gogh.

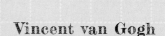

Vincent van Gogh

Vincent van Gogh (1853–1890) created more than 2,000 artworks in his short life. Van Gogh collected Japanese prints of landscapes, which inspired him to paint nature around him. His later works were made using vivid colors and energetic brushstrokes. Mostly ignored in his lifetime, van Gogh's style of painting was hugely influential on later artists.

PAINTING NATURE

Van Gogh painted his most famous works while living in the countryside in the south of France. He would walk for hours in search of the right subject to paint. Then he would carry his easel to the location and paint outside. As a result, the paint in many works contains tiny bits of plants, grains of sand, and insect footprints. One painting of an olive grove has a dead grasshopper in it!

"In all of nature, in trees for instance, I see expression and a soul." – Vincent van Gogh

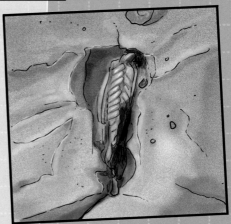

Grasshopper

WORKING TO THE END

Van Gogh was admitted to a psychiatric hospital in 1889, but his illness did not stop him from working. He painted the gardens of the hospital and the olive groves in the surrounding fields. He worked quickly, painting with big, bold brush strokes, and his paintings are full of life. In the last few months of his life, van Gogh produced a new painting every day, many of them exploding with energy and color.

Van Gogh painted the view from his hospital window 21 times. For this one, he added an imaginary village with buildings in the style of his native Netherlands.

ART AND GEOMETRY

When we look at a scene, our minds identify simpler shapes and patterns in it, making the scene more memorable. Artists often use geometry to create pleasing designs.

DRAWING WITH SIMPLE SHAPES

You can draw animals using very simple shapes. Triangles and circles can be turned into a mouse's head.

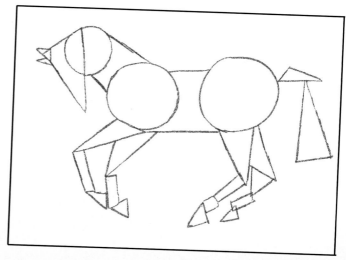

This image of a galloping horse has been created using just circles, triangles, and rectangles.

STILL LIFE

French artist Paul Cézanne (1839–1906) believed that all scenes could be composed using simple shapes such as squares, triangles, circles, and cones. Cézanne made many still life paintings in which he arranged objects into pleasing geometric forms.

Cézanne's Still Life with Flower Holder (1905) is a carefully arranged set of overlapping triangles, circles, and rectangles.

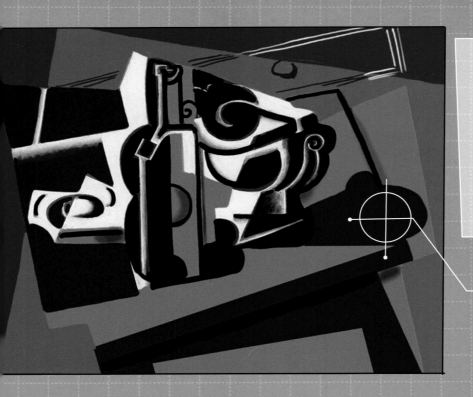

CUBISM

Inspired by Cézanne, Cubist painters played with simple shapes to create complex paintings. Their paintings included many different viewpoints all at the same time, creating fractured images.

In 1917, Spanish artist Juan Gris (1887–1927) painted this still life using simple geometric shapes. What objects can you make out in it?

ABSTRACT ART

Abstract art does not show recognisable things. Instead, abstract artists use colors, shapes, and textures to produce their images. Dutch artist Piet Mondrian (1872–1944) simplified his paintings into lines and shapes in primary colors. His aim was to depict the underlying structures of the world.

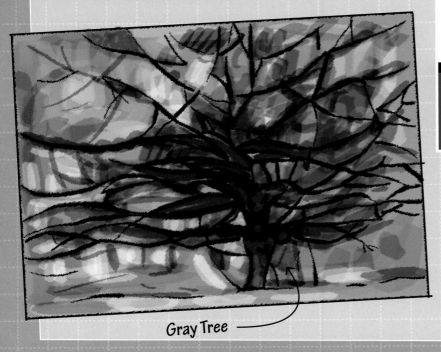

Gray Tree

Composition with Red, Blue, and Yellow

Increasing abstraction
Mondrian's painting *Gray Tree* (1911) is recognizably a tree. His later works, such as *Composition with Red, Blue, and Yellow* (1930) contained only straight lines, squares, and rectangles.

ISLAMIC ART

The Islamic Golden Age was a period between the eighth and fourteenth centuries during which art and science flourished in Muslim countries. Islamic artists developed a style that used simple geometric patterns to create stunning visual effects. Some of the finest examples of Islamic art are found in the Alhambra Palace in Granada, Spain.

Royal palace

The Alhambra was built in the thirteenth century by the Emir of Granada as a fortified palace for the royal family, known as the Nasrid dynasty. New buildings were added by later emirs and a distinctive Nasrid art style developed, featuring colorful tiles and lacelike patterns. The symmetrical patterns of Nasrid art influenced many later artists, including MC Esher (see page 31).

COURT OF THE LIONS

The Court of the Lions sits at the heart of the Alhambra. The rectangular courtyard is surrounded by four great halls. At the center of the courtyard is the Fountain of the Lions. Twelve lions look out from the round basin. Along the rim of the basin, a poem is inscribed in ornate writing. The poem praises the beauty of the fountain and the power of the lions.

The 12 lion sculptures were carved from marble.

SYMMETRICAL PATTERNS

The walls and floors of the Alhambra are covered in tiles that feature tessellation. Tessellation is created by interlocking patterns of simple shapes. The shapes display different kinds of mathematical symmetry. This means that they can be rotated or reflected while leaving the shape unchanged.

Many of the decorations at the Alhambra feature flower-shaped rosettes. The rosettes on this bench are framed by regular octagons (eight-sided shapes). They show 8-fold rotational symmetry. This means that the pattern is unchanged if it is rotated by 45°.

This pattern of batlike shapes displays 2-fold rotational symmetry, involving rotation by 180°.

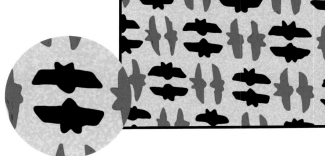

180°

COMPLEX DESIGNS

Some of the symmetrical patterns at the palace are complex collections of shapes. This decoration above an upper-floor window shows reflection symmetry. If you draw a line down the middle, one side of the line is a mirror image of the other.

Line of symmetry

RESTORING THE NIGHT WATCH

In 2019, the Rijksmuseum in Amsterdam embarked on a huge project to restore *The Night Watch*, a painting by Rembrandt van Rijn. They used cutting-edge technology to analyze the paint and made a number of surprising discoveries about how paintings change over time.

Gigapicture

The Rijksmuseum has created a giant digital image of *The Night Watch* (1642) by combining 8,439 individual photographs. Made from of 717 gigapixels (717 billion pixels), the image is the most detailed photograph ever taken of a work of art. Each individual pixel is smaller than a human red blood cell! The image can be viewed online, where you can zoom right in on the details.

DAYTIME PATROL

The huge painting (about 12 x 14 feet) depicts a group of militia guards, who had paid Rembrandt to paint them. It is commonly known as *The Night Watch* because it was assumed that the scene took place at night. However, it was in fact painted as a daytime scene. The varnished background has turned dark over time, making it look like a night sky.

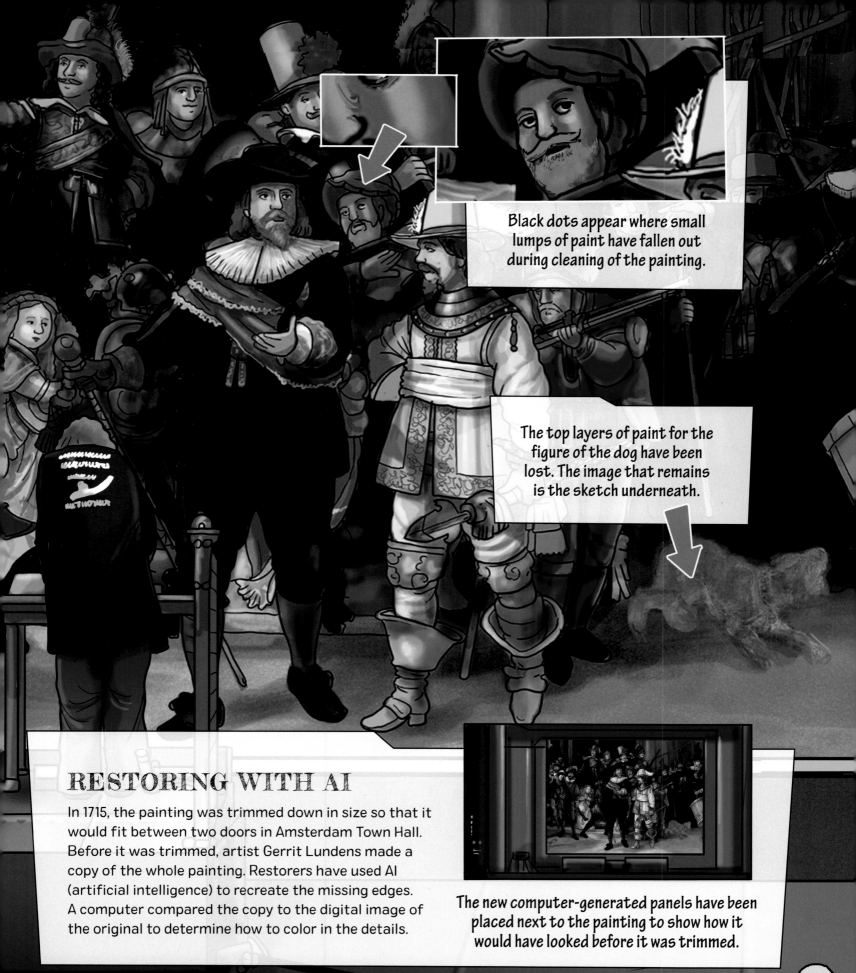

Black dots appear where small lumps of paint have fallen out during cleaning of the painting.

The top layers of paint for the figure of the dog have been lost. The image that remains is the sketch underneath.

RESTORING WITH AI

In 1715, the painting was trimmed down in size so that it would fit between two doors in Amsterdam Town Hall. Before it was trimmed, artist Gerrit Lundens made a copy of the whole painting. Restorers have used AI (artificial intelligence) to recreate the missing edges. A computer compared the copy to the digital image of the original to determine how to color in the details.

The new computer-generated panels have been placed next to the painting to show how it would have looked before it was trimmed.

FAKING IT

Art experts use a range of scientific techniques to spot forgeries. However, sometimes even the experts are fooled by a carefully made fake.

A NEW VERMEER?

Rather than copying paintings of old masters, Dutch forger Han van Meegeren (1889–1947) created brand new paintings in the same style. Van Meegeren made a number of paintings in the style of Dutch master Johannes Vermeer. These included a painting he called *The Supper of Emmaus* (1601). The painting was examined by experts and declared to be a long-lost Vermeer masterpiece.

THE REAL VERMEER

Johannes Vermeer (1632–1675) painted intimate domestic scenes of middle-class life. Only moderately successful in his lifetime, Vermeer was largely forgotten until the nineteenth century, when his paintings won fame for their use of color and light. Vermeer worked slowly and only 34 of his paintings survive, including *Girl with a Pearl Earring* (c.1665).

AGING THE PAINTINGS

To fool the experts, van Meegeren had to get many details correct. He mixed his own paints from the same raw materials that Vermeer would have used, such as lapis lazuli and lead. He also made paintbrushes from badger hair just like Vermeer. When the paintings were completed, he baked them at 200°F to harden the paint, then rolled them over a cylinder to create cracks. He added a modern plastic material called Bakelite (used to make telephones). The Bakelite ensured that the paint was as hard as it would be if the paintings were 300 years old.

TRIAL

When the war ended, van Meegeren went on trial for the sale of a national treasure to the occupying German army. However, he was able to prove that the paintings were forgeries by showing that they contained Bakelite. Van Meegeren was acquitted of collaboration with the Germans, but he was convicted of forgery. He became a hero to many Dutch people as he had swindled the hated occupying army out of a fortune.

Selling for a fortune

The experts examined van Meegeren's work using X-ray images and chemical analysis. They studied the colors under a microscope to confirm that they were the same colors that Vermeer used, and the works were passed as genuine. Many of the paintings sold for huge prices. During World War II, when the Netherlands was occupied by the German army, head Nazi leader Herman Goering bought one.

ART AND SCIENCE

Scientific ideas can be difficult to explain in words. Scientists sometimes form partnerships with artists to help them to communicate their findings in visual ways.

Maria Sibylla Merian

ILLUSTRATING NATURE

Before photography, scientists drew images of the plants and animals they studied. German naturalist Maria Sibylla Merian (1647–1717) carried out fieldwork in Suriname, South America, where she studied the lifecycles of insects. She produced a series of detailed color prints, which won her fame as both a scientist and an artist.

This illustration of cockroaches on a pineapple plant appeared in Merian's book Metamorphosis Insectorum Surinamensium (1705).

Displaying data

The British Antarctic Survey has teamed up with artists to create dramatic new ways to display the data they gather on their scientific expeditions. This image reveals the rugged mountains that lie beneath the ice in Antarctica. The image was created using data taken from the echoes of radio waves.

SCIENCE AND SCULPTURE

Chilean biologist Fernanda Oyarzun (born 1977) creates realistic sculptures of the marine animals she studies. Oyarzun uses her artwork to reveal the stunning diversity of life in the oceans. She also works with other scientists to help them to illustrate their scientific papers in new and eye-catching ways.

Crick's DNA drawing

Modern computer generated version

VISUALIZING DNA

In 1953, the geneticists James Watson and Francis Crick discovered the structure of DNA, the molecule that codes for life. For the scientific paper revealing their discovery, Crick's artist wife Odile Crick (1920–2007) drew the double-helix shape of the molecule. The drawing shows how the two strands of DNA wind around one another.

GLOSSARY

Anatomy
The scientific study of the bodies of humans and other organisms.

Artificial Intelligence (AI)
The ability of a computer to learn and to solve novel problems.

Artisan
A highly trained craftsperson who does skilled work with their hands.

Bronze
A metal alloy made of copper mixed with small amounts of tin and other substances.

Chiaroscuro
The use of boldly contrasting areas of light and shade in paintings. Chiaroscuro helps to add a sense of depth.

Collage
An artwork made with a range of different materials, such as photographs, pieces of paper and fabric.

Dissection
The taking apart of a body in order to study its anatomy.

DNA
Short for deoxyribonucleic acid. A long molecule found in the cells of all living things that carries genetic information.

Easel
A wooden frame that holds a canvas at an angle so that an artist can work on it.

Faceprint
A digital representation of a face created by a computer.

Focal point
The most important feature in a work of art, to which the viewer's eye is drawn.

Forgery
A copy of an artwork or document that is falsely passed off as an original.

Geometry
A branch of mathematics that studies the properties of shapes.

Lapis lazuli
A bright gemstone that is used to make blue pigments.

Patron
A wealthy individual who supports artists.

Perception
The way a person experiences the world. This includes qualities such as colors and sounds.

Perspective
The representation of three-dimensional objects on a two-dimensional surface.

Pigment
A substance that is added to paint to create a particular color.

Pixels
Tiny dots of light that make up a digital image on a screen.

Psychoanalysis
A form of therapy that explores a person's unconscious mind to discover the hidden causes of their mental problems.

Radio wave
An invisible form of electromagnetic radiation that has a long wavelength and low energy.

Rosette
A rose-shaped decoration.

Sfumato
A painting technique perfected by Leonardo da Vinci, in which colors and shades gradually blend with one another.

Statuette
A smaller-than-life statue that is small enough to stand on a table or a shelf.

Stylus
An instrument with a hard point that is used to write or draw.

Symmetry
A property of shapes that remain unchanged when rotated or reflected.

Vanishing point
A point at which parallel lines appear to meet in a drawing made using linear perspective.

Visible spectrum
The band of electromagnetic radiation that appears to us as visible light.

X-rays
Invisible electromagnetic radiation that has a very short wavelength and high energy.

INDEX